This Book Belongs To

_____

The Confession of Grace

Written by: Pamela Patnode

Illustrated by: Victoria Schindler

Nihil obstat: Rev. George Welzbacher. Censor Librorum. September 28, 2013
Imprimatur: +Most Reverend John C. Nienstedt, Archbishop of St. Paul and
Minneapolis. September 28, 2013

Philomena Press
providing faithful resources for faith-filled families

Philomena Press LLC
6569 Garland Lane N.
Minneapolis, MN 55311

All Bible quotations and citations come from the Catholic Study Bible: New
American Bible.

Philomena Press expresses gratitude to the United States Conference of Catholic
Bishops (USCCB) for granting permission to use Fr. Rice's Facts and Faith Series
article on going to confession. Any questions related to this information should
be directed to the USCCB Secretariat of Laity, Marriage, Family Life and Youth.
3211 4th Street NE. Washington, D.C. 20017.

For my children

And for Deacon Sam

Chapter One
Why Do You Do That?

Grace was upside down when her friend Anna approached. Eight-year-old Grace O'Malley loved hanging from the monkey bars at the park, and she smiled broadly when she spotted her friend.

"Hi, Anna!" said Grace from her upside down perch.

"Hi, Grace!" Anna replied while quickly jumping up on the bar next to her friend. "Want to come over to my house to play for a while? I can ask my mom if you can stay for dinner."

"I can't," responded Grace. "I have a meeting at church tonight. My mom says I can only play for a few more minutes before I have to go home and get ready."

"What's the meeting for?" asked Anna.

"It's for my First Reconciliation. I'm making my First Communion this year. But before we make our First Communion, we have to go to Confession," explained Grace.

"What is a first re con silly - or whatever

you said? I've never heard of that," questioned
Anna.

"Well," stated Grace, now sitting in an
upright position on top of the monkey bars,
"it's when you go to Confession for the first
time with the priest."

"Why do you do that?" asked Anna with a look of both horror and surprise.

"Well, I think it's so we can tell God that we're sorry for our sins," said Grace with a touch of uncertainty.

"So why do you have to go to a church meeting for that?" asked Anna. "Can't you just tell God that you're sorry when you're praying to Him?"

"Well," replied Grace, "we don't confess our sins at the meeting. We tell our sins to the priest when we go to Confession. I think the meeting is just to teach us how to go to Confession."

"You have to tell the priest your sins? I would

never want to do that!" exclaimed Anna. "Why do you have to do that? At my church we don't have to go to meetings and tell our pastor sins. We can just tell Jesus that we're sorry. I'm glad I don't go to your church!"

Anna swung down from the monkey bars and skipped toward home. "See you later," she called back to Grace.

Grace sat alone on the monkey bars. She was confused and a little sad. *I wonder why we do have to go to a meeting. And why do we tell our sins to a priest?* pondered Grace. *Anna's church says they don't have to. It seems easier at her church,* thought Grace.

Slowly, she got down from the monkey bars

and walked back toward her home. She had been excited about this upcoming year, but her conversation with Anna changed that. Just that morning her mom had exclaimed that this was

a very special year – to be making her First Holy Communion and her First Reconciliation. Everyone in Grace's family was joyful and excited for her. Because of all the anticipation, Grace realized she had never thought to ask why she had to do all of these things. She just did them. She was even excited about them - until she talked with Anna. Now she felt uncertain and a little afraid.

Grace and Anna lived three houses apart and they shared a park behind their homes. Grace loved playing at the park with her friend. And, she knew that Anna's family was a Christian family who was active in their church. Grace just assumed that Anna's church was the same as hers. She knew their church had a different name, but it never occurred to Grace that Anna's church might do things differently from her own. This was confusing.

Chapter Two
A Meeting at Church

As Grace opened the back door of her house, she immediately spotted her mother.

"Oh good, Honey," exclaimed her mom, "I'm glad you're back. Wash your hands quickly. Dinner is ready, and we don't want to be late for your meeting at church."

"Okay, Mom," sighed Grace as she headed

in the direction of the bathroom sink.

Grace didn't say much at dinner, and she reluctantly changed her clothes before leaving for the meeting. Once in the car, she sat and looked out the window, thinking about her conversation with Anna.

"You're certainly quiet," commented her mother as they continued their drive toward St. John's Catholic Church. "Do you feel okay?"

"Yeah," answered Grace. "I guess I just don't know why I have to go to this meeting."

"Oh, Honey!" exclaimed her mother, "I thought you were excited about all of this. What a big year this is for you! I know I'm excited! To think my baby is making her First Reconciliation and First Holy Communion!"

"I'm not a baby," grumbled Grace.

"Oh, I know dear. What's gotten into you? Are you sure you're feeling okay?"

"I'm fine, Mom," answered Grace as she continued to stare out the window.

*   *   *

Once inside the church, there was a flurry of activity. Parents and children were given name tags and folders containing a booklet and some papers. Grace recognized some of the students and smiled uncertainly as they were ushered into the meeting room.

Shortly after they were seated, Fr. Duncan walked up to the podium and began to speak.

"Welcome students and parents! I am very excited about our meeting tonight. To tell you the truth," he continued, "there is no place I'd rather be than right here with all of you."

Grace smiled. She really liked Fr. Duncan and was glad that he was the pastor of their church. With his short white hair, sparkling blue eyes, and well-fed belly, Fr. Duncan reminded Grace of a beloved grandfather. He was a jolly man who enjoyed being around people, especially children.

"The Sacrament of Reconciliation is such a wonderful sacrament, and I'm glad you will get to participate in it this year. You kids are really growing up! No more baby programs and nursery rhymes for you."

At these words, Grace glanced at her mother who smiled and winked back at her.

Fr. Duncan continued, "And because you're getting older, you're moving into the big leagues of faith. The Sacrament of Penance is a wonderful step in this direction."

"You know," Fr. Duncan continued, "God gave us this sacrament simply because He loves us. He knows that when we sin, our relationship with Him suffers. Even the little sins, the ones we call venial sins, can cause damage. It's almost as though they leave a little smudge upon our soul. What do you think would happen if we never cleaned off that smudge?"

"Our soul would get all covered in smudges," answered one little boy sitting near the front.

"That's right!" exclaimed Fr. Duncan. "Our souls would get covered in smudges. We don't want that to happen, and neither does God. That's why He gave us a wonderful way to wipe off all of the smudges. That's what

Reconciliation does. Reconciliation is a big word that means we are making things right again with God."

"Now," Fr. Duncan explained, "God doesn't give us a wash cloth and a bar of soap and tell us to get scrubbing. No, in our Catholic tradition, we have other things that work even better than soap. Prayer and the Mass are wonderful ways to clean off the stain of venial sins. And, the Sacrament of Confession is a beautiful way to get back into right relationship with God whether we've committed little sins or grave sins - the ones we call 'mortal sins'."

As Fr. Duncan continued talking about the importance of saying we're sorry for our sins whenever we've done something wrong,

Grace's mind wandered back to the monkey bars and her conversation with Anna. "At my church we don't have to go to meetings and tell the pastor our sins. We can just tell Jesus that we're sorry." Anna's words played over and over again in Grace's mind. *Why,* Grace wondered, *can't we just confess our sins to Jesus in our prayers? Why do we, at St. John's Catholic Church, go to confession with a priest?*

"And so," Fr. Duncan was saying, "you will simply sit down with the priest and share your sins with him."

At that moment, Grace's hand shot up. It went in the air so quickly that it surprised even her.

"Did you have a question, Grace?" asked Fr. Duncan.

Somewhat startled at the realization that she had interrupted his talk, Grace stammered, "Um, well, um, yes. Why can't we just tell Jesus our sins? Why do we have to tell you?"

Grace's hand fell back into her lap. Her cheeks were flushed with nervousness and embarrassment as she realized that everyone was looking at her. She heard a few coughs from some of the adults. A handful of children snickered quietly. Others stared at her in wonder.

"Oh, Grace," replied Fr. Duncan. "What an excellent question. I'm so glad you asked that." His eyes twinkled behind his glasses and his teeth shone brightly in his broad grin.

Feeling relieved that Fr. Duncan wasn't angry with her for interrupting, Grace relaxed in her seat while her mom squeezed her hand.

"How many of you here brush your teeth?" asked the good-natured preacher.

Many hands went up as the students glanced around at one another.

"That's good," stated Fr. Duncan. "It's

important to brush your teeth. Ideally, you should brush them twice a day. Sometimes, it's even a good idea to brush them more often if you've eaten something sticky or something that gives you bad breath."

A few children giggled at the bad breath comment.

"Brushing our teeth every day is very important," the priest continued. "It's also important to go to the dentist throughout the year isn't it?"

Many of the children nodded their heads. Some grimaced at the thought of their last dental visit.

"It's funny, though," continued the priest. "We can brush and floss our teeth every day and yet, when we get to the dentist and they start working in our mouth with their tools, they always manage to find things we missed. They clean off stains, plaque, and anything else that has built up on our teeth. They can also help repair any damage that has been done. This thorough cleaning from the dentist is important. It helps our teeth remain healthy and clean.

"The Sacrament of Reconciliation," continued Fr. Duncan, "is somewhat like the visit to the dentist. To keep our souls healthy, we do need to tell Jesus that we're sorry for our sins. We also need to apologize to our family and friends when we've hurt them. In fact, I try to tell Jesus I'm sorry every night before I go to

sleep. In prayer, I think about how the day went, and I ask Jesus to forgive me for all of the sins I committed that day. My daily prayer to Jesus is somewhat like my daily tooth brushing. It is necessary and important for a healthy soul.

"Unfortunately, there may be times in life when we commit a very grave sin – a mortal sin. Mortal sin is very dangerous to our soul and our relationship with God. It actually has the potential to blot out the life and light of sanctifying grace from our souls. However, do you want to know something? God still loves us. Even when we are at our worst, God loves us, and wants us to turn our hearts back to Him. The Sacrament of Penance helps us to do that. It lets the light of Christ's mercy and life back into the death and darkness caused by mortal sin. And, in the same way that the dentist may give you some tips on keeping your teeth healthy, the priest can give you tips on keeping your relationship with Jesus strong and healthy. And so, it's not an *either/or* type of thing. We don't *either* say we're sorry to Jesus in prayer *or* go to Confession. No, as Catholic Christians, we get to do both!"

Grace smiled. She thought what Fr. Duncan had said made perfect sense. Why would we not want to do both? We do both with our teeth, after all, by brushing daily and going to the dentist. And our teeth aren't even as important as our souls. She felt very good, again, about the idea of making her First Reconciliation.

Chapter Three
Back at the Park

Grace was in high spirits for a number of days following the meeting at church. As the youngest of the family, Grace had already watched her other siblings prepare for the Sacrament of Reconciliation. Now, armed with a better understanding of why it was necessary, Grace felt proud and excited that her day to participate in this sacrament was arriving soon.

The fall months passed quickly as the family kept busy with school work, housework, and many outside activities. Soon, Thanksgiving arrived crisp and clear.

While her mother busied herself in the kitchen, preparing for the Thanksgiving meal, Grace grabbed her coat and headed toward the park. Her friend Anna was already there, attempting to beat a distance record by jumping off of the swings.

"Hi, Anna!" called Grace as she sped toward her friend.

"Umpf," grunted Anna as she landed flat on her back in the sand. "I was so close to beating my record. The mark in the sand is right here."

"Let me try!" exclaimed Grace while grabbing the swing's chains and hopping on. Grace pumped her legs with great effort, trying to gain height for the record breaking attempt.

"Okay," yelled Anna. "That's high enough! Ready? One, two, three, jump!"

Grace released her grip on the swing and sailed, feet first, toward the far reaching mark of champions. She landed, falling forward to her knees.

"Did I beat it?" asked Grace.

"Let's see," said Anna. "It looks close. I think it's a tie. Yep, look here, I think you tied the record."

"Wow!" exclaimed Grace. "That's the farthest I've ever jumped!"

"Great," replied Anna. "Let's go on the monkey bars now."

The two girls climbed quickly to a perch on top of the monkey bars. Once there, they decided to prepare Olympic bar routines that were scored by imaginary judges from around the world. Easily they flipped and turned and swung, being careful to keep their toes pointed, so as not to get any deductions from their score.

After many routines and imaginary gold medal victories, the girls sat, once again, atop the monkey bars and talked about the upcoming holidays and plans their families were making. They chatted about relatives coming to town, gifts for which they were asking, and special holiday concerts that they were a part of. It was during this conversation that Grace mentioned her upcoming Confession.

"Oh," exclaimed Anna. "I forgot about that. Are you nervous?"

"Not really," replied Grace. She then went on to share with Anna some of the things Fr. Duncan had told them about the sacrament.

"That makes sense," replied Anna. "But

does the Bible say that? At my church, our pastor says we should only do those things that the Bible tells us to do. I've never read anything in the Bible about confessing sins to a priest."

Grace didn't know what to say. She had no idea what the Bible said regarding Confession. In fact, she had never even considered this question. After a pause she simply said, "I don't know. I'll have to find out."

At that moment, Anna's mother called from the back door. "Come in, Anna! It's time to go to Grandma's!"

Anna swung down from the bars and waved to Grace as she left. "Have fun today, Grace!"

"Good-bye, Anna!" replied Grace.

Again, Grace sat alone atop the monkey bars, feeling confused. *Was the Sacrament of Confession something found in the Bible?* she wondered. *What if it wasn't?*

Grace swung down from the bars and walked toward home. Her enthusiasm for the upcoming sacrament was once again dampened. *I guess this is what Fr. Duncan meant when he said no more baby games and nursery rhymes,* thought Grace. *This 'now that you're older stuff' is hard to figure out.*

Chapter Four
A Conversation with Fr. Duncan

Thanksgiving passed and the Advent season began with hopeful anticipation. Radio stations, shops, churches and homes resounded with Christmas carols, holiday greetings, and a joy that bespoke the season.

In addition to decorating their home for Christmas, shopping for gifts, and attending holiday festivities, Grace and her parents spent time working through her materials for the Sacrament of Penance.

For this sacrament, St. John's always planned a very special event for the children. A Saturday morning in Advent was set aside for the students and their families. Numerous priests from the many Catholic churches in the area came to hear the confessions of the faithful. As the youngest of five children, Grace had been to this event four times already (as an observer), and she knew what to expect. First, upon arriving, she and the other children who were first time participants would turn in their completed materials. They would then be invited into the church to sit with their family. A beautiful service would be prepared involving music, prayer, and an examination of conscience.

When Grace was younger, she didn't know what "examination of conscience" meant. She could remember asking her mom what is was. Now she understood that it was taking a good look at her own conscience to recognize the sins she had committed. Grace knew that it was one of the steps in preparing for Confession with the priest. She understood that to actually confess sins out loud, you needed to know what you were going to say. The examination of conscience gave you the time and the tools to figure that out.

As the day of her First Reconciliation approached, Grace became more and more uncomfortable. Anna's question burned in her mind. *What did the Bible have to say about Confession?* Grace wondered. She knew that she wasn't an expert Christian, but she knew enough to recognize that what the Bible said was important.

Grace wanted to find out what it said (or didn't say) about Confession, but she didn't know how. She was a pretty good reader, but a quick look through the Bible assured her that she'd never be able to find the answer on her own. With all of the small type, strange names, and big words, she could barely read most of the pages.

After some deliberation, Grace decided to ask her mom.

"Mom, what does the Bible say about Confession?" asked Grace.

"What do you mean, Darling?" replied her mother.

"I mean, Anna says that at her church, the pastor says they should only do what the Bible tells them to do. She asked me if the Bible says we're supposed to go to Confession."

"Oh, I see," answered her mother. "You and Anna have had some good discussions about this haven't you? I think Anna has asked a very important question. And, I think it would be good for both of us to learn the answer. Let's go see Fr. Duncan and ask him. That way we'll know we're getting the right answer. I'll give him a call and see if we can meet with him."

*   *   *

As Grace and her mother drove toward St. John's, Grace was filled with a mixture of emotions. First, she was a little excited to see Fr. Duncan's office. She had never been in a priest's office before and she wondered what it would be like. Maybe his desk would be shaped like an altar, and maybe his computer would be sprinkled in holy water. She wasn't sure. She was also a little nervous. She wondered if he would be frustrated with her for asking so many questions. Her stomach felt a little knotted as they pulled into the parking lot.

Once inside, Grace looked around the

friendly priest's work space. His desk was not shaped like an altar, it looked like a regular wooden desk. He did have a crucifix hanging on the wall, a bottle of holy water on a filing cabinet, and a rosary near his keyboard, but other than that, it looked like a regular office.

Fr. Duncan shook their hands warmly, and his

genuine smile reassured Grace that he was not frustrated with her. The beloved priest invited Grace and her mom to sit in the two chairs near his desk and offered them something to drink.

Once seated, Fr. Duncan smiled again and asked if they had any questions. Grace's mom said, "Well, Fr. Duncan, Grace and her friend, Anna, have been having some wonderful conversations about Grace's upcoming Confession. Anna asked Grace an important question the other day, and we thought it would be good to get the answer from you. Grace, would you please share Anna's question with Fr. Duncan?"

Grace looked at her mom and then at Fr.

Duncan. "Well, Anna asked if the Bible tells us that we should confess our sins to a priest. At Anna's church they don't do that."

"I see," replied Fr. Duncan. His face was thoughtful as he looked at Grace and then her mother. After a pause he said, "Grace, you have asked me some very important questions. These are questions that all Catholics should be asking. If you don't mind, I'm going to write these down – the one you asked at the meeting, and the one you're asking me today. I want to make sure that I explain these questions and their answers to everyone at St. John's. That's how important these questions are. You and Anna are doing a great thing for our church by having these conversations. I'm glad you and Anna are friends. And, I'm glad you've asked me these questions."

Grace smiled, feeling relieved that Fr. Duncan wasn't angry. She also felt a little surprised at just how pleased he was with her questions. She didn't really think her conversations with Anna were very special, but apparently Fr. Duncan thought they were.

"Grace," Fr. Duncan continued, "the Bible has a lot to say about the Sacrament of Reconciliation. God loves us. And, He knows that sin can damage our relationship with Him. He wants us to always be close to Him, so He gave us many ways to repair any damage in our relationship, or wash away any smudges from our soul. The Sacrament of Reconciliation is one of those ways.

"I could spend the entire afternoon sharing with you Bible verses and Church doctrine that explain why we confess our sins the way we do in the Catholic Church. However, I have a feeling you don't have the entire afternoon to spend with me, so I'm going to give you one important verse and some information to help you understand the Sacrament of Confession. Does that sound good to you?"

Grace nodded. She was a little relieved that he was not going to keep her there all afternoon. And, one verse and some information, she thought, would be enough to help her understand.

"The first Scripture verse I want to share with you comes from John's Gospel. Being that I'm the pastor of St. John's, I think it would be good to start out with St. John's Gospel, don't you agree?" Fr. Duncan grinned.

Grace returned his smile and nodded.

"Grace, when Jesus was alive on earth, He did many things. He cured the sick, He prayed,

He fasted, He fed people, He taught people about God, He loved, and He forgave sins. One example of Him forgiving sins occurs in the story of the paralytic. Do you remember the story of the paralyzed man whose friends lowered him through the roof of the house?" (Luke 5:17-26)

Grace nodded.

"Good," replied Fr. Duncan. "Well, before He cured the man, Jesus forgave the man's sins. It's important to remember all that Jesus did because this verse I'm about to tell you relates to Jesus' actions in a very important way."

Grace sat up a little straighter in anticipation of the verse.

Fr. Duncan opened his Bible and said, "In

John 20:21-23, Jesus (after He rose from the dead) met with His disciples. He said to them,

'Peace be with you. As the Father has sent me, so I send you.' And then He breathed on them and said to them, 'Receive the Holy Spirit. Whose sins you forgive are forgiven them, and whose sins you retain are retained.'

"This verse is very important, Grace. First, Jesus tells His disciples that He is sending them out into the world in the same way that God had originally sent Jesus. That means that they will need to do all of the things that Jesus did when He was alive on earth. And, in giving them the Holy Spirit, they would have the necessary grace to be able to do those things.

Grace, do you remember what Jesus did?"

Grace nodded and replied, "He loved people and cured people and did miracles and forgave sins."

"That's right," exclaimed the jovial pastor. "After His resurrection, Jesus asked the disciples to do all of those things. And, through the power of the Holy Spirit, He gave them the grace and authority to be able to do them.

And, just in case they had any doubts about the forgiving sins part, Jesus clarified this point by telling them *'Whose sins you forgive are forgiven them, and whose sins you retain are retained.'*

"The disciples became the first bishops, the first Catholic priests, and Jesus gave them the authority to forgive sins through the Holy Spirit. Now Grace, I have a question for you. How could the disciples of Jesus forgive sins if no one came forward, told them their sins, and asked for forgiveness? Or, how could I forgive your sins if you didn't come to me with contrition and ask for forgiveness?"

Grace looked at Fr. Duncan. "I don't know,"

she replied. Slowly, understanding began to come over her. "I mean, I guess you can't really forgive anyone's sins unless you know what their sins are."

"Right!" exclaimed Fr. Duncan. "Jesus gave the disciples the authority to forgive or not to forgive the sins of others. Well, the only way the disciples could know if they should forgive or not forgive would be if that person came forward and confessed. For the disciples to justly forgive (or refuse to forgive), they needed to know three important things. First, they needed to know the sins of the person. Second, they needed to know whether or not the person was truly sorry for their sins. Third, they needed to know whether or not the person intended to try to stop doing the sin. The only person who could give this information to the disciples would be the sinner himself. Something as important as offering forgiveness or withholding forgiveness is not left up to guessing. That makes pretty good sense doesn't it?"

Grace nodded. She considered all that Fr. Duncan had shared with her. It did make sense. The Bible says that Jesus gave the authority to the disciples to forgive or retain the sins of others. The only way they could do that, however, would be if a person came forward and confessed their sins. Likewise, our priests today, through apostolic succession and the power of the Holy Spirit, have the authority to retain sins or forgive them. The only way they can do so, however, is if someone comes forward to confess their sins. Only through the Sacrament of Confession can a priest know for which sins we seek forgiveness, whether or not we truly feel sorry for our sins, and whether or not we plan (with God's help) to change our behavior.

As they rose to leave, Fr. Duncan reached into his desk drawer and pulled out a crucifix on a chain.

"Grace," he said, "I want you to have this." And, he handed her the beautiful gift. "When I was a young boy," he remarked, "I asked questions just like you. Back in the little church where I grew up, our pastor was a pretty busy guy. He didn't always have time to answer my questions. We had a Deacon, however, who became my friend. Deacon Sam always seemed to have time for me. Once, when I was visiting with him in his office, he handed me a crucifix on a chain that I could wear around my neck. 'Take this,' he said to me. 'Whenever life gets tough or you need an extra hand, just squeeze this crucifix and know that Jesus is at your side.' I still carry that crucifix all these years later. And, just like Deacon Sam did for me, I'd like to give you your own special crucifix as a

reminder that Jesus is with you wherever you go."

Grace admired the unexpected gift with wide eyes. "Thank you, Fr. Duncan," she exclaimed. "Thank you very much!"

Fr. Duncan's eyes danced as he looked down upon the child and her mother.

On the ride home, Grace's mother commented that she thought the meeting was very valuable. "In fact," she added, "I'd like you to share with your father and your siblings what you learned today. At dinner tonight, would you tell them? I think our whole family should know this information."

Grace agreed while she admired the crucifix in her hands.

Chapter Five
Grace's First Confession

Grace stretched, opened her eyes, and then got out of bed. Today was her big day. She walked down the hallway toward her parents' room. She could hear the water running in the shower and realized that her dad was already up.

"Good morning, Darling," said her mother,

who was still lying in bed. "You're sure up early."

Grace climbed into bed beside her mom and rested her head on the pillow next to her mother's.

"I'm excited for today," said her mom. "Are you?"

"Yes," Grace nodded.

"You sure have done a lot of work to prepare for this sacrament. I'm proud of you," said her mother. "And, do you know who else is proud of you?"

"Dad?" asked Grace.

"Well, yes," replied her mom. "Your dad is proud too. But I was thinking of someone else.

I believe that Jesus is proud of you. I really do. It took courage to raise your hand during the meeting and ask a question in front of everyone like you did. And, it took time and effort to go to Fr. Duncan's office the other day and talk with him. If everyone had your courage and put time and effort into their faith like you, I think we'd have fewer problems in our world. Yes, Grace, I believe Jesus is proud of you. And your dad and I are too."

Grace smiled as her mom hugged her tightly.

*　　*　　*

Once at church, the service unfolded as Grace had envisioned. It was very similar to the Reconciliation services she had been to in the past. However, the big difference this time was that, instead of watching her family members get in line to individually confess their sins to the priest, she would be joining them, and confessing her sins as well. *Fr. Duncan was right,* she thought. *This does feel like a big*

step. 'The big leagues of faith' he had called it.
Yes, she was growing up, and she was glad.

As the time drew near for her to stand in line, awaiting her turn for Confession, Grace knelt with her family in the pew. She bowed her head and began to pray. As she did, she held the crucifix Fr. Duncan had given to her. Grace

knew, as Fr. Duncan had said, that Jesus was walking beside her on this new and exciting faith journey. It was certainly proving to be an interesting journey, different than she had ever imagined. As she prayed, she thanked God for her family, thanked God for Fr. Duncan, thanked God for her friend Anna, and thanked God for the Sacrament of Confession. She was glad she could clean off any smudges she had on her soul and stay close to Him. Grace closed her eyes and considered her sins. Then, she rose, and stepped in line for Confession.

*   *   *

The smile on Grace's face as her family left the church reflected how she felt in her heart.

Her soul felt happy and light and clean!

Just as they were about the leave the church, Fr. Duncan approached and shook Grace's hand. Grinning, he said, "Congratulations."

The sun outside was shining and her heart was singing. Yes, it was a wonderful, wonderful day!

For More Information

This story gives just a small amount of information regarding the Catholic Church's teachings on the Sacrament of Reconciliation and Penance. To learn more, please see the resources listed below.

The United States Conference of Catholic Bishops has a website that includes a tremendous amount of information related to Catholic teaching. Their web address is: www.usccb.org. For information specific to the Sacrament of Reconciliation and Penance please go to: www.usccb.org/prayer-and-worship/sacraments/penance/

The Catechism of the Catholic Church is an excellent resource to learn more about the Catholic faith. Article Four in the Chapter on the Sacraments of Healing contains a wealth of information. Please note, when looking for information in the *Catechism of the Catholic Church*, paragraphs are numbered. The index will list the paragraph number (rather than the page number) of the highlighted topic.

Dr. Scott Hahn is a noted Catholic professor and author. His books provide much information on different aspects of Catholic teaching. One book that discusses the Sacrament of Reconciliation is: *Signs of Life: 40 Catholic Customs and Their Biblical Roots.*

The Process of Going to Confession

If you have not been to confession in a while, do not worry! The priest will be more than happy to walk you through the process. Some general steps are listed below. However, do not feel anxious about following a procedure. Rather, turn your heart to Christ and allow the priest to guide you!

Following is an excerpt taken from "How to Go to Confession" by Fr. Larry Rice, CSP (USCCB website):

In my experience as a confessor, I often encounter people who aren't comfortable, or who don't quite remember how Reconciliation works. So here are Fr. Larry's tips for a good confession.

1. Know what it is you want to confess. Spend some time reflecting on your life, and examine your conscience so you know why you need God's forgiveness.

2. Find a confessor you're comfortable with. If you want more anonymity than you think you'll get with a priest at your own parish, go to a neighboring parish. Lots of people do.

3. If you have lots to say, or if you will want more than a five minute conversation, don't just get in line on a Saturday afternoon. Call a priest and make an appointment. It's better if you don't feel rushed.

4. Relax. If it's been a while, or if you're nervous, or you don't remember how to proceed, just tell the priest. He'll reassure you, and walk you through the process.

5. "I don't remember the Act of Contrition." Not to worry. After you receive your penance, and before the prayer of absolution, you need to pray an Act of Contrition. If you don't have one memorized, you can say a prayer in your own words telling God you're sorry for your sins, and that with His help you'll try to do better.

6. Go regularly. Many people find it helpful to see the same confessor every few weeks. With regular confessions, particularly face-to-face, your confessor can help you look at the patterns of your life, not just individual sins.

Two popular forms of the Act of Contrition Prayer:

Act of Contrition

O my God, I am heartily sorry for having offended You, and I detest all my sins, because of Your just punishments, but most of all because they offend You, my God, who are all-good and deserving of all my love. I firmly resolve, with the help of Your grace, to sin no more and to avoid the near occasion of sin.

Act of Contrition

My God, I am sorry for my sins with all my heart.

In choosing to do wrong and failing to do good, I have sinned against You whom I should love above all things.

I firmly intend, with Your help, to do penance, to sin no more, and to avoid whatever leads me to sin.

Our Savior Jesus Christ suffered and died for us. In His name, my God, have mercy.

Amen.

Acknowledgments

My children graciously helped me compose this manuscript, allowing some personal experiences to be re-told. The way they live out their faith is an inspiration to others, most especially to me.

My husband is my constant support and best friend. Without his encouragement and business expertise, this book would not be in print.

A special thank you to Jennifer Ladendorf for her careful review of the manuscript. Her insight and input was of tremendous value to me.